A New Level

UNDERSTANDING PENTECOST

STEPHEN MANLEY

Cross Style Press

A NEW LEVEL: UNDERSTANDING PENTECOST
© 2018 by Stephen Manley

First Published 2005
Revised Edition 2018

Published by Cross Style Press
Lebanon, Tennessee
CrossStyle.org

All rights reserved. No part of this book may be reproduced in any form without prior permission from the publisher, except for brief quotations.

Unless otherwise indicated, all Scripture quotations are taken from the New King James Version®. Copyright © 1982 by Thomas Nelson, Inc. Used by permission. All rights reserved.

Edited by Delphine Manley

ISBN-10: 0-9987265-5-9
ISBN-13: 978-0-9987265-5-7

Printed in the United States of America.

CrossStyle.org

CONTENTS

1	What a Day! *Acts 2:1*	7
2	The Joy of the Law *Acts 2:1*	17
3	Avenues of Unity *Acts 2:1*	27
4	The Sound from Heaven *Acts 2:2*	39
5	The Filling *Acts 2:2*	49
6	To Be Seated *Acts 2:3*	59
7	Filled With What? *Acts 2:4*	69
8	The Spirit's Mouthpiece *Acts 2:4*	79

A NEW Level

1
WHAT A DAY!
ACTS 2:1

    The celebrations of the Jewish nation were always focused on God Jehovah. These celebrations commemorated the significant things their God had done. God had not only delivered them from their enemies, but He had also given great provisions for their living.

    The Feast of the Passover was an exciting celebration which actually continued into the Feast of Pentecost. The Jews called Pentecost "the concluding assembly of the Passover." What took place in the Passover was so powerful and long reaching it flowed into the Feast of Pentecost. There was a combination of things being celebrated during these Feasts. It started out with the offering of a Lamb. The entire ceremony was family oriented. Each family, numbering at least ten, would tell the story of how God delivered them from Egyptian bondage. They would highlight how the Death Angel passed over (Passover) their homes because the blood of the sacrificed lamb had been placed on their doorposts. This happened on the fourteenth day of the first month, which was always a Friday.

On Saturday, the fifteenth, which was the Sabbath Day, they celebrated the Feast of Unleavened Bread. During the next seven days they ate only unleavened bread. This was a remembrance of the march out of Egypt land. The next day, the sixteenth, was the first day of the week. It was the Feast of the Firstfruits, and it was the beginning of the great harvest. The people of Israel were to bring a sheaf of the firstfruits of the harvest to the priest, marking the beginning of the offering of the firstfruits. Fifty days later the harvest was completed. Two leavened loaves of the finest of flour were baked and brought to the priest as the firstfruits of the completed harvest. So the first sheaf offered at the Passover and the two leavened loaves at Pentecost marked the beginning and the end of the grain harvest, and sanctified the interval between as the whole harvest or Pentecostal season.

Do you see that God was ushering in the New Covenant? The Passover lamb was the symbol and means of Israel's deliverance from Egypt. It marked the beginning of everything good God had promised the Israelites. The only reason they had a land of plenty and a great harvest was the blood of the lamb. On that very day of the Passover celebration, at that very moment when the High Priest offered the official Passover lamb, hanging on a cross, Christ gave up His right to live. The veil of the temple was ripped from top to bottom. All that the Passover pointed to and symbolized was now fulfilled.

The day following the crucifixion was the Sabbath Day and the Feast of the Unleavened Bread. This was referred to as the "bread of affliction." The yeast, which in time would permeate the bread, was eliminated. The

Israelites were to remember the haste of the journey from Egypt. It was a symbol of the journey of our Lord as He made His way in death to the full payment of sin. Here was the clash of good and evil in the greatest of battles. Everything would rise and fall on the outcome of this journey. Would the Savior emerge victorious? Even if He escaped, would the foe actually be defeated and redemption for mankind be grasped?

The next day was the first day of the week. It was the Feast of the Firstfruits. The harvest had begun and the first sheaf was brought to the priest. What a day this was! It is the very day God raised Jesus from the dead! Paul wrote, **But now Christ is risen from the dead, and has become the firstfruits of those who have fallen asleep** (1 Corinthians 15:20). The resurrected Lord is the Firstfruit of a great harvest which was be completed on Pentecost.

This is all one great event from the Biblical view. In our society we segment and departmentalize, but in the Jewish culture it was not so. The writers of the Bible viewed the crucifixion, resurrection, ascension and Pentecost as God's one redemptive movement. It was all connected. God did something very big in the crucifixion. It would manifest its firstfruits in the resurrection, but would come to the full harvest on the Day of the Feast of Pentecost.

Therefore it is absolutely impossible to understand the impact of the Day of Pentecost without looking at the many elements of the "firstfruits" and embracing their concept.

FIRST IN SEQUENCE

The Greek word translated "firstfruits" is the combination of a prefix and a basic root word. The prefix is a primary particle which denotes "from." The root word means "to begin." It denotes the first point of time according to the context. It may have to do with creation (Hebrews 1:10; Matthew 19:4, 8), the first appearing of Jesus (Luke 1:2; John 15:27), or the ministry of Christ (Acts 1:2).

Our basic interest is with the firstfruit of the crucifixion. We have discovered the Day of the Feast of the Passover focused on the offering of the sacrificial lamb, enabling Israel's deliverance from the Death Angel. On that day as the High Priest was in the Holy Place with the official sacrifice lamb, Jesus was hanging on the cross. At the exact same moment the priest's knife touched the throat of the lamb, ***Jesus cried out again with a loud voice, and yielded up His spirit*** (Matthew 27:50). Could this have been an accident or coincidence? Was not God bringing to pass all He had promised?

The next day was the Sabbath Day. We are given details of the activities of man during that day. The ***chief priests and Pharisees gathered together to Pilate*** (Matthew 27:62). They broke their law by traveling beyond a Sabbath Day's journey. They also broke their defilement law by going into Pilate's palace. What was so important to them? They were anxious to seal the tomb with a Roman seal and prevent the disciples from stealing the body of Christ. However, we have very little knowledge of what took place in the spiritual realm during this time. What was Jesus doing? The mystery of the tremendous invasion into the demonic territory is beyond us. Jesus paid the equivalent of our entire eternity in hell. Yet, hell could not contain Him. This day was the Feast Day of Unleavened Bread. It was the celebration of the march out of Egypt and was surrounded by the miracles of God. Jesus experienced His own Feast Day of Unleavened Bread for us.

The next day was Sunday, the Lord's Day. It was the Feast Day of Firstfruits. It was on this day Israel presented to the priest the sheaf of grain from the beginning of the harvest. It was a symbol of all that was to come as the harvest was completed. It was a promise of hope concerning the provision of God for His people. What a celebration it must have been! Christ, the Lamb, had been crucified and brought forth firstfruits. He made the journey into death and hell. Now the firstfruit, the resurrection, was given.

Jesus was the first sheaf of grain. Let me remind you what Paul wrote, **But now Christ is risen from the dead, and has become the firstfruits of those who have fallen asleep** (1 Corinthians 15:20). He is the first in the sequence. He is the first One to appear in the full potential of all the crucifixion would produce. If you were wondering, what would be the full and complete product of the crucifixion, you need no longer wonder. Jesus is the Firstfruit.

Paul went on to state, **And He is the head of the body, the church, who is the beginning, the firstborn from the dead, that in all things He may have the preeminence** (Colossians 1:18). In this sense He is the first, the *firstborn*, the *beginning* (root word of *Firstfruits*) from which all creation has received its norm. The average has been established again. It is Jesus!

FIRST IN SUBSTANCE

This is the second element. The root word in *firstfruits* has a philosophical application. It denotes the original material from which something has evolved. This "something" is determined by the context of the source. When the sheaf of grain was presented to the priest, it was the substance of the source. It represented the original material of the grain plant which entered into death that the sheaf might be produced. The rest of the harvest was to be of this same original matter.

Jesus spoke forcibly on this issue. Several Greeks came to Jerusalem to worship at the feast. They confronted Philip, desiring to speak to Jesus. We are not absolutely sure as to their intentions. However, it seems reasonable they were interested in securing Him as a new leader among the Greeks. Perhaps they wanted Him to start a new college in Athens. He would be the greatest teacher the world had ever known. He could spend His time writing books and influence the world forever. Jesus did not even need to pray about such a proposition. **But Jesus answered them, saying, "The hour has come that the Son of Man should be glorified,"** (John 12:23). In John's Gospel account this is always a reference to the crucifixion of Christ. Jesus confronts the Greeks with the crucifixion.

He gave a physical illustration with His description. He said, **"Most assuredly, I say to you, unless a grain of wheat falls into the ground and dies, it remains alone; but if it dies, it produces much grain,"** (John 12:24). It is an illustration from nature highlighting the firstfruits. One grain of wheat dies to produce a harvest of the original material in many grains.

Jesus is the first in the sequence. He represents the quality of the complete harvest which is to come. He is the representative of the rich grain, the golden kernels which will flow as the harvest is completed. We are again forced to use "prototype" language. Everything produced from this point on will be compared with Jesus. Is it the same material? Does it come from the same source? Is it the same texture, fiber and substance?

Do you realize we are surrounded by a lot of religious plastic? If you simply drive by the churches of our day, you would not recognize anything is different. The buildings are shaped the same. The songs have the same words and express the same theme. There are many of the same rules and activities. But when you stop the car and actually get close, it is not the same substance. It is synthetic in nature. It does not have the aroma of Christ. The texture is radically different. The material of the grain of wheat is not present. Its death did not produce the harvest. It came from another source and is not acceptable. The Firstfruit of the crucifixion is the standard. It is far beyond imitating Jesus; it requires participation in the material until we are the same. What would Jesus do (WWJD)? This is not the question. At best it is a beginning question. We cannot simply attempt to be like Jesus. The issue is not that we try to be like Him, but we are to be sourced by Him. The substance, the original material, from which He is made, is now to be ours. We are to be *partakers of the divine nature, having escaped the corruption that is in the world through lust* (2 Peter 1:4).

What exactly is this original material? How can I experience it? Where can we find it? We must go back to the Prototype. He is the Firstfruit of the crucifixion.

What is the source which has brought this to pass? It is the fullness of the Holy Spirit!

FIRST IN SURETY

Before we look at this third element, we want to review the pattern which God has been following. The Feast of the Passover focuses on the sacrificial lamb. It is fulfilled in the crucifixion of Jesus. *The next day John saw Jesus coming toward him, and said, "Behold! The Lamb of God who takes away the sin of the world!"* (John 1:29). Our crucified Christ is the fulfillment of the Feast of the Passover.

Following the Good Friday fulfillment was the Sabbath Day. It was the celebration of the Feast of Unleavened Bread which symbolized the haste, hardship, and miracles connected with the flight out of Egypt land. This was fulfilled in the burial and mystical activity of Christ during His death.

This was followed by the Feast of Firstfruits, taking place on Sunday, the Lord's Day. It marked the beginning of the harvest which would continue to be completed on the Day of the Feast of Pentecost. Israel was to bring to the priest the first sheaf of grain from the harvest. It contained the substance or material characteristic of the remaining harvest. The resurrected Lord is the Firstfruit of the harvest. Paul stated it this way, *But now Christ is risen from the dead, and has become the firstfruits of those who have fallen asleep* (1 Corinthians 15:20). He is the norm, the prototype, of all who are to follow.

The harvest continued for fifty days. It climaxed on the Day of the Feast of Pentecost. The actual word Pentecost means fifty. This feast was called The Festival of Weeks because it was celebrated for seven complete weeks, or fifty days, after the Feast of the Passover (Exodus 34:22). It was also called the Festival of the Harvest because it concluded the harvest of the later grains (Exodus 23:16).

The sheaf of grains (firstfruits) was offered to the priest on the first day of the week (Sunday) after the Day of the Feast of the Passover. Again, it marked the day of the harvest's beginning. Fifty days later the harvest was completed. On this Day of the Feast of Pentecost, two leavened loaves with the finest flour were baked and brought to the priest as the firstfruits of the completed harvest. So the first sheaf offered at the Passover marked the beginning of the grain harvest, and the two unleavened loaves at Pentecost marked its end.

These two fresh baked loaves brought at the completion of the harvest symbolized the Holy Spirit given to us. The outpouring of the Holy Spirit on the Day of the Feast of Pentecost is the completion of the harvest or crucifixion. This is what God planned all the time. This is the goal, dream and vision of God for you. If the crucifixion had ended the life of Christ there would have been no harvest. The firstfruits of the resurrection would never have been presented. We would have been forgiven through the shedding of blood, but this was not the complete dream of God for us. God's dream was not completely fulfilled with the crucifixion and resurrection. There was something more He wanted to accomplish than forgiving us and allowing us to live forever.

Even though the crucifixion, resurrection, and ascension took place, God still had not accomplished His goal. He forgave us, gave us eternal life, and crowned

Jesus King, but our destiny as determined by God was still undone. The completion of the harvest, the two baked leavened loaves, is none other than God living within us. We can now be possessed by the very nature of God. He will not settle for anything less than this. Do you see how big this is?

It is bigger than you have ever dreamed! In speaking of this the Apostle Paul wrote, *Now He who has prepared us for this very thing is God, who also has given us the Spirit as a guarantee,* (2 Corinthians 5:5). The Greek word translated *guarantee* means "a pledge or earnest." It is part of the purchase money on property given in advance as security for the rest of what is due. Do you see what this means? The two fully baked loaves given at Pentecost are simply a down payment. What we experience in the fullness of the Holy Spirit now is only a surety. It is not that God has something new and different for us. No! It is the same material and original substance found in Christ. What we experience in the nature of God now is only a fraction of what He is going to continue to do in and through us. He will source our daily living as we are in intimate relationship with Him.

You do not want to miss this! You must be filled with the Spirit. Whatever obstacles are in your way, allow God to remove them. Experience the cross that you might experience His life.

2

THE JOY OF THE LAW
ACTS 2:1

In this passage, Luke distinctly pinpoints the exact day in which God fulfills His promise. The disciples have been waiting in Jerusalem for the "Promise of the Father." They are minus the full details of this eminent outpouring of the Holy Spirit, but they are following God's instructions to wait. The Holy Spirit comes and pours Himself on these open seekers on **the Day of Pentecost** (Acts 2:1). It is very important to understand how the Old Testament patterns were simply **shadows** of the realities of God's plan for His people.

We need to consider these verses. In speaking of the priests, the author refers to them as those ***who serve the copy and shadow of the heavenly things, as Moses was divinely instructed when he was about to make the tabernacle. For He said, "See that you make all things according to the pattern shown you on the mountain,"*** (Hebrews 8:5). ***For the law, having a shadow of the good***

things to come, and not the very image of the things, can never with these same sacrifices, which they offer continually year by year, make those who approach perfect, (Hebrews 10:1). In referring to the requirements of the Old Covenant, Paul wrote that these ***are a shadow of things to come, but the substance of Christ*** (Colossians 2:17).

It is for this reason we are investigating ***the Day of Pentecost*** in light of the Jewish celebrations. Let me remind you the Day of the Feast of the Passover took place on Friday. It was a remembrance of the day when the Death Angel passed over the Hebrew people who were enslaved in Egypt. The blood of the sacrificial lamb was used for the deliverance of their firstborn sons. This lamb was a constant reminder of the promise of the Messiah. Jesus surrendered His life on the cross at the very moment the high priest offered the official Passover lamb on that Good Friday.

The next day was the Sabbath Day. It was the celebration of the Feast of Unleavened Bread, commemorating the difficult journey out of Egypt. This was the symbol of the journey of Christ in His burial experience. All of the unknown portions of this involvement remain a mystery to us. However, the next day was the first day of the week. It was the celebration of the Day of the Feast of Firstfruits. The beginning of the harvest was acknowledged as the people presented a sheaf of grain to the priest. This is the shadow of the resurrection of our Lord. He is the firstfruits of the great harvest to come (1 Corinthians 15:20).

The harvest continued for a period of fifty days. It climaxed on the Day of the Feast of Pentecost. Two baked loaves of bread made from the finest flour and yeast were presented to the High Priest. It was the symbol of the fulfillment of the harvest and the provision of God for His people. During those fifty days Jesus ascended to the right hand of the Father. We are given only brief insight into the activities in the heavenly realms. He serves as the great High Priest who offers His sacrifice once and for all. He receives the Promise of the Father in order to pour the blessing upon us. The completion of the dream of God for His people takes place. It is the climax of the harvest.

However, in the Jewish celebration of the great Day of the Feast of Pentecost, there was an additional element. It was the celebration of the law. The Day of the Feast of Pentecost not only celebrated the completion of the physical harvest, but also commemorated the giving of the law, the spiritual harvest. The time period from the passing over of the Death Angel in Egypt to the experience on Mount Sinai when Moses received the law from God was fifty days. The Day of the Feast of Pentecost was sometimes called by the Jews, "The Joy of the Law."

I would like for you to think of the tremendous parallel of all of this. In the Old Testament the fulfillment of the great harvest in the spiritual sense was the giving of the law of God. In the New Testament the fulfillment of the great harvest was the indwelling of God. In the Old Testament, the Day of Pentecost was the writing of the law of God on tablets of stone. In the New Testament the Day of Pentecost was the writing of the law of God on the hearts of men. In the Old Testament the climax of the movement of God was the establishment of the nation of Israel, the organization of the government, and the giving of the law. In the New Testament the climax of God's dream is the Kingdom of God, the crowning of its King, and the empowering of its rule. The Kingdom of God is within you (Luke 17:21). God and man have moved into such intimacy that the empowering, sourcing flow of the nature of God has indwelt man. It is the fulfillment of the dreams of God for us!

There are distinctions between the Old Covenant Pentecost and the New Testament Pentecost. It is the law contrasted with the indwelling of the Spirit of Christ. We need to consider these distinctions together.

CONCENTRATION

We do not have the time or space to investigate the entire Old Testament concerning this issue. From the days of the Judges, down through the experiences of captivity, a central issue was the backslidden condition of the people of Israel. It was always focused on breaking the law of God. But something happened to the people of the Kingdom of Judah during the last captivity. They came back to Jerusalem and rebuilt the temple and the walls of the city. They rediscovered the law of God. There was a rededication of their lives to God's law from which they would never again stray.

This was the time period in which the group called Pharisees began. They concentrated on the law of God. They interpreted the law of God by their oral traditions. This accelerated during the four hundred years that God was silent, the period of time between the Old and the New Testaments. They had nothing left but their law. It became their only focus. The Day of the Feast of Pentecost was a celebration of their focus.

The law had become their light in the dark hours. It was

their guide through difficult circumstances. The only measurement they had of right and wrong was contained in the law. The highest position in their social status was an interpreter of the law. These people outranked all other political positions. All rights and wrongs were determined by the law. Judgments in the Jewish courts were decided by the interpretation of the law. All actions were measured by the law. The very basis of their security in relationship to the favor of God was the law. To remove the focus of the law would be to leave them with nothing. Their focus was the law, the law, and the law!

The outpouring of the Spirit of Jesus came on the very day when they were celebrating their focus on the law. How radical it was! God Himself was breaking through all of the structure, ceremonies, and doing, in order to present Himself. It was a total focus on the Person. The Book of Acts is an account of a people who are absolutely captivated with the Person of Christ. What they knew in the external has become internal. The fellowship they experienced in the flesh has moved to the Spirit. He became the center of everything happening in their lives.

The intensity of the Jew's focus was on the law. Think of how their lives must have been filled with it. It was the measure and judge of everything they did. If the law was lost, then everything they held close was gone. The law was their total focus. NOW shift that intense focus to the person of Christ. He has come to indwell them. Everything is being determined by Him. How do I know I am righteous? He is my righteousness. How do I know I am doing the right thing? I respond to the "poieo-ing" of His presence. How do I know I love properly? His love is flowing through me.

As I once argued for the law, now I embrace Him. As once theology was the great issue of my life, now He is my supreme love. As once I was filled with religious doing, now I respond to His movement. As once I ministered for Him, now He ministers through me. I used to serve Him, now He serves through me! The greatest example in the Scriptures of this shift is the Apostle Paul. He wrote, ***And I advanced in Judaism beyond many of my contemporaries in my own nation, being more exceedingly zealous for the traditions of my fathers*** (Galatians 1:14). Can you see him on his horse riding to Damascus? He has papers in his hands giving him the right to destroy men, women, and children who are called Christians. But his testimony continues, ***But when it pleased God, who separated me from my mother's womb and called me through His grace, to reveal His Son to me,*** (Galatians 1:15-16). It was a shift from the law to the Person. As he had been focused on the law, now he was focused on Jesus.

The Day of Pentecost is now a great celebration of our focus. We are centered on Jesus. We have nothing else if He is not our concentration. We are left lifeless and empty without Him. We have no way to measure where we are or to sense security without Him. He is our all in all!

CIRCUMFERENCE

There is a second contrast between the Old Covenant Pentecost and the New Testament Pentecost. The circumference which established the limits of the lives of the people of Israel was contained within the law. We must go back to "boundary language." The boundary which established the fences beyond which the children of Israel were not to go was the law. This was the constant cycle in the Old Covenant. Israel was not willing to live within the boundaries of the law and experienced the consequences of it.

The message of the Old Testament is one of relationship. God's dream for mankind from creation, to the fall, to the redemption, is all about relationship. In the Old Testament it is highlighted as "Covenant." The basic Hebrew word translated "covenant" in the Old Testament appears two hundred and eighty times. There is some debate among scholars as to the origin of this word. Some have said it comes from a custom of eating together (Genesis 26:30; 31:54). Others have suggested the idea of cutting an animal (Genesis 15:18). The preferred meaning of this Old Testament word is "bond." A covenant is two or more parties bound together.

The Old Testament presents many covenants between two equal parties; this means that the covenant relationship is bilateral. Both parties sealed the bond by vowing, often by oath. They had equal privileges and responsibilities within the covenant. But the covenant between God and Israel is different. It is unilateral. This basically means that the covenant only involves or is affected on one side, or it is performed or undertaken by only one side. It obligates only one of two parties. God initiates the covenant. Israel is the recipient not a contributor. Israel is not expected to offer elements to the bond or covenant; Israel simply accepts it as offered. Israel is to keep its demands and to receive the results that God, by oath, assures them He will not withhold.

The law is the boundary within which Israel is to abide

and receives the benefits of this relationship. We see the picture of what took place when they stepped outside the law. The benefits of the covenant protection and provision were immediately removed. They had gone beyond the circumference of the relationship.

The Day of Pentecost in the New Testament was a shift in the boundaries of the covenant. God was moving His people to a new level of relationship. The covenant was going to take on an exciting new aspect. The Old Covenant Pentecost celebrated the law. But through the years the law had taught the reality of sin. The law was a schoolmaster. ***Therefore the law was our tutor to bring us to Christ, that we might be justified by faith. But after faith has come, we are no longer under the tutor*** (Galatians 3:24-25). Romans chapter seven is Paul's description of a person who is living in the Old Covenant, celebrating "the joy of the law." It could not be done. Mankind, who lived out of his own resource, was incapable of staying within the boundaries of the law, thus the provisions of the covenant were lost.

But now the boundary of the law of the Old Covenant has moved from external to the internal (Hebrews 10:16). It is no longer on tablets of stone but in the hearts of men. We are no longer motivated by provisions or benefits of a covenant, but by relationship. ***For the love of Christ compels us, because we judge thus: that if One died for all, then all died; and He died for all, that those who live should live no longer for themselves, but for Him who died for them and rose again*** (2 Corinthians 5:14-15). Therefore the actual boundary of the covenant has shifted from law (doing) to Christ.

Jesus said, ***"Do not think that I came to destroy the***

Law or the Prophets. I did not come to destroy but to fulfill (Matthew 5:17). The boundary of the covenant is no longer keeping a list of rules (doing), but embracing the Person. God has initiated the covenant; it is unilateral. I bring nothing to the covenant. It is not my part and His part. It is all His part! In embracing Christ, I am sourced with life to live. The law brought nothing but death (Romans 7:10). Christ brings nothing but life! The single source of God's dreams for me is in the embrace of the Spirit of Christ. I am to live within the boundaries of His Person. I am constantly responding to His provision in me.

COMMUNICATION

We come now to the third contrast between the Old Covenant Pentecost and the New Testament Pentecost. It is communication. It is amazing how in the Pentecost of the New Covenant a new language was formed and a new vocabulary emerged. It was an absolute necessity that this would take place. This new level of experience and intimacy with Christ demands new expression. There will have to be new imagery to picture the relationship. The Old Testament law language will no longer be adequate.

Jesus introduced this idea in the great manifesto of the Kingdom of God, the Sermon on the Mount (Matthew 5-7). He used a contrast in the middle of the sermon. It was a contrast between, ***You have heard that it was said to those of old*** and ***But I say to you.*** The old was about not committing murder; but the new is about not being angry (Matthew 5:2-22). The old was about not committing adultery while the new is about lust in the heart (Matthew 5:27-28). The old was about no divorce in the family; the new is about faithfulness (Matthew 5:31-32). The old was about not getting even with your brother; the new is about not resisting (Matthew 5:38-39). The old was about not hating your enemy; loving everyone is the new (Matthew 5:43-44). The language has changed!

The old language was about Hebrews, Jews, Israelites, chosen ones, children of Abraham and isolation. It was about Gentiles, Samaritans, and defilement. The new language is explosive. New language like "the body of Christ" began to give a new picture of intimacy with each other and Him. The language of the Church was born. We became the bride of Christ (Ephesians 5:25-32), born from above, sons of God, and joint heirs with Christ. We are the temple of the Holy Spirit which is made up of living stones (Ephesians 2:22; 1 Corinthians 3:16; 1 Peter 2:5). We moved from not being allowed to even pronounce the name of God Jehovah to the constant use of the name of Jesus. We went from God isolated in the Holy of Holies to living in His presence. He was inaccessible; but now we embrace Him. It is a whole new language.

Do you recognize that all of the new language is related to the person of Christ? It is absolutely impossible to have this language when the focus is on the law. Now we are the bride of Christ, joint heirs with Christ, and the temple of the Spirit of Christ. Let us live in intimacy with Him!

3
AVENUES OF UNITY
ACTS 2:1

They were all with one accord in one place. All the commentaries focus on these two phrases as meaning they were all assembled together in a single location. The commentators attempt to reveal where this place might have been, although there is often disagreement. They argue about whether it was the one hundred and twenty disciples present, or whether it was only experienced by the twelve apostles. It amazes me that no one seems to deal with the real issue. Why would Luke go to so much trouble to double state what would have been otherwise very obvious to any one reading the passage?

To further complicate the issue there is the Greek word which is translated ***with one accord.*** In verse fourteen of chapter one, this same translation is used for one Greek word. The issue is whether it is the same Greek word in both verses. Most Bible scholars believe they are not the same in the original Greek text, and the word used in verse one of chapter two should be changed to a translation reading, *together*. It appears the earliest Greek manuscripts have two different Greek words for these verses. The Greek word translated **with one accord** (Acts 1:14) has the idea of likeminded. They were thinking and feeling the same way. The Greek word translated *together* (Acts 2:1) is more of an emphasis on the fact they were physically together in one location.

Our consideration is whether this really changes anything. Something has already happened to these disciples as a group. The resurrected Jesus has captivated them and their new focus has elevated them above all strife and differences. We cannot forget how often, before the crucifixion, there was strife and division among them. Jesus was faced with not only strife from outside the group, but from within. They were divided over issues of position in the coming Kingdom (Matthew 18:1). They were competitive when others outside the group were successfully ministering (Luke 9:49). There was a major upset when two disciples who were brothers sought to secure the right and left hand positions for themselves (Matthew 20:24). Racial division rose to the forefront when a Samaritan village refused to give them lodging (Luke 9:52). It was such a heated issue, they wanted to **command fire to come down from heaven and consume them** (Luke 9:54). They all disagreed with Jesus over the cross style (Matthew 16:22). Mighty arguments were staged concerning this proposal. On and on it goes! Now things are very different. What has happened to the disciples to cause such a radical change?

In chapter one Luke highlights the disciple's new focus. It is the Resurrected Lord. They spend forty days with

Him (Acts 1:3). His person, heart and vision capture them. He becomes so large in their eyes that everything else diminishes. This sets the stage for the outpouring of the Spirit of Jesus, and the New Covenant is established. All contention ceases. They are *with one accord* and then Pentecost happens.

Now let us return to our passage (Acts 2:1). The Greek word which is translated *with one accord* is used ten times in the Book of Acts. It is only used one other place in the New Testament (Romans 15:6). The gathering of the disciples *in one place* (Acts 2:1) is not one of the ten usages of this Greek word. However, this gathering is certainly surrounded by the Greek word translated *with one accord.* It is used to describe the waiting period in Jerusalem before the Day of Pentecost. *These all continued with one accord in prayer and supplication, with the women and Mary the mother of Jesus, and with His brothers* (Acts 1:14). Luke gives us a summary description of the one hundred and twenty disciples during the seven to ten day period between the ascension of Christ and the Day of Pentecost.

When the Day of Pentecost happened, Peter preached a powerful sermon (Acts 2:14-40). About three thousand converts were added to the group of one hundred and twenty (Acts 2:41). In the summary description of what was taking place among this enlarged group, Luke uses this same Greek word. *So continuing daily with one accord in the temple, and breaking bread from house to house, they ate their food with gladness and simplicity of heart* (Acts 2:46). Luke emphasizes this concerning the disciples both before and after Pentecost.

There is an event recorded by Luke immediately after

Pentecost. A lame man *whom they laid daily at the gate of the temple which is called Beautiful* (Acts 3:2) was healed. This great miracle created a platform for Peter to deliver a message about Jesus, and hundreds of people responded (five thousand men, Acts 4:4). The leaders of Israel were greatly distressed and put the apostles in jail for the night. The next day they gave them a hearing. After warning and threatening them *not to speak at all or teach in the name of Jesus* (Acts 4:18), they released them. Immediately the apostles returned to the gathering of the early church and reported all that had been said to them. Here is how the early church responded to the report of the threats: *they raised their voice to God with one accord and said: "Lord, You are God, who made heaven and earth and the sea, and all that is in them,"* (Acts 4:24). Again Luke emphasizes the linkage of the believers even as it expanded to a larger group.

Should we not interpret our passage in light of this fact? The actual text says, *When the Day of Pentecost had fully come, they were all with one accord* (together) *in one place* (Acts 2:1). Again, notice the double emphasis! Luke states they were *together.* In addition he adds *in one place.* In light of what Luke has already told us (Acts 1:14) and what he will tell us (Acts 2:46; 4:24), we must understand the content of *together in one place* to mean *with one accord.*

It is also important to note the Greek word translated *with one accord* is a combination of two Greek words. The first word is the Greek word translated *together* as in our passage (Acts 2:1). The second Greek word has to do with passion as if breathing hard. So the Greek word used in our passage (Acts 2:1) is the basis of *with one accord* used in the other passage. This combination of two words is very expressive. It signifies that all their minds, affections, desires, and wishes were concentrated on one object; every man's focus had the same end in view. They had but one desire. There was no person uninterested, none unconcerned, none lukewarm; all were in earnest; and the Spirit of God came down to meet their united faith. This kind of uniting gives to the Holy Spirit a powerful platform for Divine action in our world!

There is nothing to indicate that this removed their differences. The experience of *one accord* is not the absence of strife over differences but the concentration on one object which brings the passion of the individuals into unity. They did not all suddenly like the same color, crave the same dessert or drive the same make of car. Nothing had changed among them except their overwhelming passion for one object. In our previous studies we discovered the object of their affections. The resurrected Lord had captivated them. He spent forty days sharing with them about the dreams of the Kingdom of God (Acts 1:3). He became so large in their vision that nothing else seemed to matter. Other things were still there, but these things diminished in their eyes. Their love for Christ overtook all other concerns.

Being in *one accord* demonstrated itself in various areas. Their absolute obsession with the resurrected Christ began to reveal itself in the essential spiritual avenues for the flow of the Holy Spirit. Their unity manifested itself not in liking the same music or enjoying the same hobbies, but in the areas where the Holy Spirit needed to affect their world. What are these areas?

PRAYER

One specific area of flow is prayer. This was utilized by the Holy Spirit prior to the outpouring on the Day of Pentecost. The unity manifested in this area seems to have been a key factor in releasing the hand of God for the outpouring. Luke describes the one hundred and twenty disciples in the "waiting" time in Jerusalem. This is not a retreat setting where they were isolated from conflict. They were in the heart of Jerusalem spending their time in the temple with the leadership of Israel (Luke 24:53). They were dwelling in the very seat of the movement which crucified Christ. It was here ***these all continued WITH ONE ACCORD in prayer and supplication, with the women and Mary the mother of Jesus, and with His brothers*** (Acts 1:14).

The flow of the Holy Spirit through the avenue of prayer was not something only experienced in preparation for Pentecost. Prayer is emphasized repeatedly among this group throughout the Book of Acts. The Greek word translated ***prayer*** is used nine times as a noun and sixteen times as a verb in the Book of Acts. What is really revealing is that this word is used eight times in the Gospel accounts as a noun and forty-seven times as a verb. It is startling to realize in the Gospel accounts the disciples are never seen doing this word. The only One who actually experiences this word ***prayer*** in the Gospels is Jesus. He is either talking about it or doing it.

Can you imagine the first time the disciples get together in the upper room and experience ***prayer?*** Even before Pentecost through Christ there was a new access to the spiritual realm. The Old Testament, old covenant, had never provided anything like this. Then as they experienced Pentecost, **prayer** was widened and deepened in their lives. But understand it was not getting on their knees and reading a list of requests to God. It was not the rehashing of memorized phrases repeatedly. There was actually fellowship and living in the presence of God. **Prayer** had become "practicing His presence." They were living in a new God awareness!

These early disciples were **with one accord** in the realm of **prayer.** This did not mean they were all praying for the same thing, but they were all in intimate fellowship with Jesus. The awareness of His presence had become such a focus they were elevated above all their differences. If there is strife among us, is it not evident that we do not have the awareness of His presence? Unity in this area releases the power of God as it did in the Book of Acts. Strife destroys intimacy with Jesus in the individual and also in the corporate body of Christ. The moment we are not in intimacy with Him we are left to our own devices. We become man produced rather than God sourced. We cannot afford strife!

PARTNERSHIP

Another area utilized by the Holy Spirit to flow His influence through them was the unity experienced in partnership. What an experience it must have been to see hundreds of people in the temple giving their lives to Christ and being filled with the Holy Spirit. After the outpouring of the Holy Spirit, Peter confronted those in the temple area with an explanation of this great event. The disciple group suddenly was enlarged to over three thousand individuals. *Then fear came upon every soul, and many wonders and signs were done through the apostles* (Acts 2:43).

While these happenings must have been wondrous, what took place afterward was beyond comprehension. They were **continuing daily WITH ONE ACCORD in the temple, and breaking bread from house to house, they ate their food with gladness and simplicity of heart** (Acts 2:46). There was a unity that possessed them which can only be expressed in the full understanding of the Greek word ***koinonia*** (partnership).

The content of **with one accord** in this setting is explained by the proceeding verses. The disciples (enlarged group) **had all things in common** (Acts 2:44). Again this was not about liking the same kind of music or the same athletic competition. Luke gives us the details. He writes, **and sold their possessions and goods, and divided them among all, as anyone had need** (Acts 2:45). Think of the kind of unity which would remove all materialistic barriers. What could possibly take place within an individual or group of people that would bring them to this level?

This is a strong example of partnership (***koinonia***). This Greek word comes from the root word meaning "to do business." It is far beyond fellowship or even companionship. This word includes those ideas along with linking together in an enterprise. The disciples had been pulled into the heart of Christ. They were all in a single business; it was Christ. The Kingdom of God, Christ within you had become so huge in their lives there was nothing else. All other concerns diminished in light of this one great enterprise. Christ received their entire energy, desires, passion and obviously materialism. They were in unity in the flow of the Holy Spirit through the enterprise of the heart of God.

Is this not the key element to how they won their entire world in seventy years to Christ? This kind of unity brought the flow of the Holy Spirit which empowered and sourced an evangelism which swept people into the Kingdom. Nothing could stop such evangelism. The power of the Holy Spirit flowed through this unity with signs and wonders. Everything needed to convince their world of Christ was available to them. In the midst of the lack of organization, education, money and buildings, they simply swept their world into the Kingdom of God.

What could stop such a thing from happening among us? The great hindrance to such a movement is strife. Strife is produced by a focus on minor issues. When we argue about methodology, style of worship, even theology, we destroy the avenue through which the Holy Spirit can release His power. We are again back to our own abilities. Strife is the evidence that we have lost focus on Him. The sin of our world has never stopped or hindered the church. Persecution has only increased the effectiveness of the church. Outside threats have never destroyed the body of Christ. It is from within we are ruined. The moment we are no longer totally His we find ourselves belonging to minor issues which always produce division.

PRAISE

There is a third avenue of unity which became an avenue for the Holy Spirit's flow. It is the avenue of praise. A tremendous evangelistic gathering occurred from the miracle which happened at the gate of the temple called Beautiful (Acts 3:2). At the hour of prayer, Peter and John went to the temple and were encountered by a lame man. The power of God healed the man astounding everyone. Peter used this as an opportunity to share Jesus with the gathering. There was an additional five thousand men who believed in Christ (Acts 4:4). The leaders of Israel arrested the disciples and left them in jail for the night. The next day they threatened them regarding preaching in the name of Jesus (Acts 4:18).

Upon their release the apostles made their way to the expanded group of believers. They **reported all that the chief priests and elders had said to them** (Acts 4:23). What a terrible position in which to be! These are the same leaders of Israel who crucified Christ. This is a life threatening situation. How will the early church respond? *So when they heard that, they raised their voice to God WITH ONE ACCORD and said: "Lord, You are God, who made heaven and earth and the sea, and all that is in them,"* (Acts 4:24). They responded in praise and worship to their great God! Did you notice the unity in this worship?

As the passage develops, it is clear this expanded group of disciples is focused on the greatness of God. They are absolutely convinced of Jesus (Acts 4:27). They believe the life of Christ was a fulfillment of the plan of God which is now going to continue through them (Acts 4:28-30). As they spoke these declarations in unity, *they were all filled with the Holy Spirit, and they spoke the word of God with boldness* (Acts 4:31). It was through this kind of unity in praise and worship to God that the Holy Spirit was able to move!

Exactly what was their level of unity? *Now the multitude of those who believed were of one heart and one soul; neither did anyone say that any of the things he possessed was his own, but they had all things in common* (Acts 4:32). They were **with one accord** in their focus on Christ and the fulfillment of the plan of redemption in spite of any obstacles. Their praise and worship was not focused on music, beat, or environment, but was captured by Him. All styles of worship faded in importance. There was no manipulation of the crowds but a unity of focus on Him.

This avenue of worship and focus was so strongly used by the Holy Spirit that all who did not join in this focus were struck dead (Acts 5:1-10). *And believers were increasingly added to the Lord, multitudes of both men and women,* (Acts 5:14). Do you see how central unity was in the flow of the Spirit? All strife is destructive to the flow of the Spirit of God and must be eliminated. There is no chance of revival when we are divided. Walls and barriers are the supreme hindrance to the movement of the Spirit both in our individual lives and the corporate body of Christ. God give us unity!

4

THE SOUND FROM HEAVEN
ACTS 2:2

Is there any way to describe God's awesome gift to the world? God had been speaking through the generations of time, but now He chooses to climax it all in a new dynamic movement. The Spirit of Jesus moves within the lives of human beings. The Day of Pentecost has *fully come.* It is time to reveal it to mankind. Are there any adequate words?

Luke uses naturally familiar and physical elements to give us a feel for the occasion. He speaks of the wind and the fire (Acts 2:2-3). Wind and fire always emit excitement, but we must resist the temptation to become enthralled with these occurrences. Luke specifically writes, **And suddenly there came a sound from heaven, AS OF a rushing mighty wind, and it filled the whole house where they were sitting** (Acts 2:2). There was no **rushing mighty wind,** but only what sounded like wind. **Then there appeared to them divided tongues, AS OF**

fire, and one sat upon each of them (Acts 2:3). There was no *fire,* only that which appeared as fire.

In my attempt to go past the physical representations which illustrate what is happening, I was astounded to find that both wind and fire point to the issue of "communication." In Luke's second illustration, there were ***divided tongues*** which focus on communication of speech. As demonstrated in the next verse, Luke writes, ***And they were all filled with the Holy Spirit and began to speak with other tongues, as the Spirit gave them utterance*** (Acts 2:4). The obvious result of the fullness of the Holy Spirit is that of communication.

Luke's first illustration of the event is the phrase; ***there came a sound*** (Acts 2:2). To hear this sound was to think of a roaring, blasting wind. However, as the sound fills the room, it is connected to communication and the speaking which is happening. ***And when this sound occurred, the multitude came together and were confused, because everyone heard them speak in his own language*** (Acts 2:6).

This revelation forced me to a definite conclusion. In every movement of God His motivation is communication. I am unable to find an event in God's actions or presence where communication is not predominate. ***There came a sound,*** but it was not for the mere sake of noise. God is making known a startling and amazing truth.

I investigated the Book of Acts to discover the places where the fullness of the Holy Spirit takes place without communication. Such an occasion does not occur. The Book of Acts is about the coming of the Holy Spirit, communicating truth to us! Let me list a few of these references for our study.

> *But you shall receive power when the Holy Spirit has come upon you; and you shall be WITNESSES to Me in Jerusalem, and in all Judea and Samaria, and to the end of the earth* (Acts 1:8).
>
> *And they were all filled with the Holy Spirit and began to SPEAK with other tongues, as the Spirit gave them UTTERANCE* (Acts 2:4).
>
> *Therefore being exalted to the right hand of God, and having received from the Father the promise of the Holy Spirit, He poured out this which you now see and HEAR* (Acts 2:33).
>
> *Then Peter, filled with the Holy Spirit, SAID to them...* (Acts 4:8).
>
> *When they had prayed, the place where they were assembled together was shaken; and they were all filled with the Holy Spirit, and they SPOKE the word of God with boldness* (Acts 4:31).
>
> *And those of the circumcision who believed were astonished, as many as came with Peter, because the gift of the Holy Spirit had been poured out on the Gentiles also. For they heard them SPEAK with tongues and magnify God* (Acts 10:45-46).

There are many more Scriptures we could add to the list, but space does not allow. Communication of truth always surrounds the fullness of the Holy Spirit. Repeatedly, as the apostles speak the truth of God, the Holy Spirit comes upon others. **Sound** seems to be a consistent element in the movement of the Spirit of Jesus.

Having established this premise, let us investigate

the ***sound from heaven, as of a rushing mighty wind*** (Acts 2:2). Let me remind you of the great occasion when God instituted the law for His people. He made an appearance before Israel on Mount Sinai. As the people gathered at the base of the mountain, here is what took place. ***Then it came to pass on the third day, in the morning, that there were thunderings and lightnings, and a thick cloud on the mountain; and the sound of the trumpet was very loud, so that all the people who were in the camp trembled*** (Exodus 19:16). All of this was a prelude to the speaking of God as He gave His law to Moses! It is not about noise; it is all about communication.

One is immediately drawn to remember that when God came in the flesh, He is referred to as the "Word." ***And the Word became flesh and dwelt among us, and we beheld His glory, the glory as of the only begotten of the Father, full of grace and truth*** (John 1:14). The incarnation was definitely about communication. Jesus was and is the speaking of God. His coming is God's attempt to tell us something. Communication from God has now arrived at a new level. We have moved from thunderings and lightnings, accompanied by trumpets, to God becoming flesh. What a revelation!

But there is more. God takes us to an even higher level. He re-establishes His indwelt presence within! What He has intended for man from the beginning is now coming to pass. It is not about emotional feelings, nor power to do miracles. God raises His communication with man higher still. ***"I will put My law in their minds, and write it on their hearts; and I will be their God, and they shall be My people,"*** (Jeremiah 31:33). This is definitely a new level of communication. And how astounding is it that the very first description of this happening is ***sound***? God indwells man with communication!

We need to carefully note that this is a ***sound FROM heaven.*** Its primary meaning is "out of" or "from." It is the little Greek word "ek." It is used to speak of objects which were in another time before this time. If the object was simply on, by, or with another, but not in it, then the Greek word "apo" is used. The ***sound*** which was heard was not by or around heaven; it was actually in heaven. What was heard on the Day of Pentecost is the same communication which is present in heaven itself! The communication of the Holy Spirit has its origin in heaven. The music of heaven is now being heard on earth! The message shared in heaven is now being communicated on earth! The attitude which is a part of the ***sound*** of heaven is now being felt on earth!

You need to carefully think through what this means. The ***sound*** taking place on the Day of Pentecost is not on the circumference of God's existence. It is not outside the person of God and adjusted by Him for us. This sound comes from the interior of the heart of God. This is what His dwelling place sounds like. It is not a watered down version or an anemic substitute of His communication. God opened up the heart of His being to us. In the fullness of the Spirit we experience the inner thoughts of God. The beloved music of God now plays within us. His wisdom runs through our lives. God is communicating with us!

But here is what is so startling about the word ***sound***. It is only used four times in the New Testament. It is the Greek word "eechos." From it we get our English word "echo." While the actual Greek word is not used, it is connected with Paul's trip to Rome. In the midst of the storm *they took soundings and found it to be twenty fathoms; and when they had gone a little farther, they took soundings again and found it to be fifteen fathoms* (Acts 27:28). The sailors suspected they were getting close to land. The Greek word translated *soundings* means that the sailors suspected that there was an echo coming from the land.

The author of the Book of Hebrews uses the Greek word "eechos" one of the four times. He discusses the giving of the law on Mount Sinai. He compares the old covenant with the new covenant. He tells us that we have not come to the *mountain that may be touched and that burned with fire, and to blackness and darkness and tempest* (Hebrews 12:18). He goes on to describe the scene of Mount Sinai; *and the sound of a trumpet and the voice of words, so that those who heard it begged that the word should not be spoken to them anymore* (Hebrews 12:19). The echo coming from Mount Sinai was a communication so powerful that the people of Israel could not tolerate it. They requested Moses to go and get the message and bring it back to them. The giving of the law was an echo of the holiness of God. God reflects Himself in the law He communicates.

You remember the great "love chapter" of Paul's writings (1 Corinthians 13). He begins by saying, *Though I speak with the tongues of men and of angels, but have not love, I have become sounding brass or a clanging cymbal* (1 Corinthians 13:1). If one speaks without love, there is no communication. He is not echoing the heart of God, but the sound of a gong banging in the temple. The communication of the Gospel is far beyond the speaking of certain words. It must be the echo of God's heart. The Gospel is not communicated through doctrine or theology, but through those individuals who have become a reflective echo of God's heart, for God is love. This is what happened on the Day of Pentecost.

Another place this same Greek word is used is in connection with Jesus. The ministry of Jesus had expanded throughout Galilee. Luke states, ***And the report about Him went out into every place in the surrounding region*** (Luke 4:37). Here our Greek word "eechos" is translated ***report.*** What was being spoken on the streets about Jesus was an echo of the activities and message He had been sharing with them. The report being given was a reflection of the real life of Christ.

One of the delights of childhood is the echo of the mountains. In certain places sound reverberates between two mountains. If we yell at the top of our lungs in these unique places we will hear our words repeated back to us. It is as if the mountains are talking to us! But the mountains only repeat what we say. They do not produce the sound, nor form the statements. They simply echo our words!

Luke attempts to describe the indwelling of the Spirit of Christ within us by use of this physical illustration. The fundamental purpose for which God created mankind is now being fulfilled. Man is to be an echo of the very essence of God. Mankind is not to produce or mimic the sound. He is not to be an imitation of the sound. God created mankind to be a sounding board from which the nature of His person could be reflected and heard. The actual voice of God is to echo from within our being.

Do you grasp how essential this is? A life lived less than this is a forgery. Whatever is produced by us is phony regardless of how good and great it may appear. Ministry sourced by our talents, developed skills, and personality types is counterfeit. It may attract people and produce church growth, but it does not grow the Kingdom. Any expression of our personality and discipline is a fake! We are to be an expression of the Divine Love, a display of God's very nature. We do not love for His sake; He must come and love through us. We are to be an echo of His heart!

Oh, to be filled with the *sound* of His presence! I am repulsed by how often I have been a fraud, an impostor, or a replica. I have filled my life with excuses as to why this is my lot. Christianity is not about right and wrong. Christianity is about Him. If one could discover the right thing to do, go and do it, he would still go to hell. Christianity is not about doing the right thing. God calls each of us to be an echo of His person.

Christians witnessing as described in the Book of Acts won their world in a matter of seventy years. They were filled with the *sound* which was the essence of heaven. They became an echo of the voice and heart of God. Jesus forcibly demonstrated this before them. He did not call them to do what He did, only to be what He was. He was the echo of the Father. Anyone who viewed Him was viewing the Father. He did not produce His own life nor walk His own path. He was the reflection of the face of the Father. For the first time in history we discover what God sounds like. We hear the echo of His voice through the life of Christ.

Now we see the purpose of the crucifixion, resurrection, and ascension events. The ultimate purpose is not to get us into heaven or to forgive our sins. God wants to restore us until we properly echo His being. All that echoes through Jesus now echoes through us. It is the fullness of the Spirit of Christ.

One can quickly see the kind of surrender this demands. It requires a complete crucifixion of all self-will. There can be no mixing of my part and His part. This is not about my doing and His helping. This is not even about my repeating what He says and does. This is death to all that spills from me. I must cease to be the source of the echo. This is difficult for all of us. Most of us have spent years developing and cultivating our skills, talents and abilities. We have been shaping our lives so we can be acceptable. We take great pride in our wise accomplishments, and we acknowledge that God has certainly helped us. But what Luke describes is far beyond this. He calls us to renounce all self-reliance. Everything that comes from us must cease. Who will become available to God in such a manner? Remember everything but this is simply a replica, a forgery, a phony, a fake, a fraud, and an impostor. Who will be an ECHO?

5

THE FILLING

ACTS 2:2

Luke establishes a contrast between chapters one and two of the Books of Acts. He uses It is in this contrast to highlight the turning point in the history of the Kingdom of God. Many believe the birthday of the Church is contained within this new phase of His redemptive plan. In chapter one the disciples are reminded of the promise of the Father; in chapter two they are actually receiving the fulfilled promise! In chapter one, they are waiting for the coming of the Holy Spirit; in chapter two He comes. In chapter one the disciples were equipped by Jesus; in chapter two they are empowered by the Spirit of Christ. In chapter one the resurrected Savior ascended; in chapter two the Spirit descends. In chapter one the disciples are being spoken to; in chapter two they are speaking in languages they do not even know. Something is being birthed in this great event! The Kingdom of God has come to a new level of life!

It seems to be significant that Luke is using three different Greek words for "filled" in the first four verses of chapter two. The first two are closely related to each other, thus forming a presentation of two major ideas. Our study will be filled with the comparison of these two concepts.

In Luke's opening statement he writes, **when the Day of Pentecost had fully come** (Acts 2:1). As he continues his description of this great event, he speaks of a **sound from heaven** which **filled the whole house where they were sitting** (Acts 2:2). The Greek word translated **fully come** and **filled** are formed from the same basic Greek word. It has the meaning of "to fill a vessel." The focus of the word is on a container being filled with content. It focuses on something outside coming to be inside. In the Greek translation of the Old Testament, the authors speak of God filling the heavens and the earth (Jeremiah 23:24). This term is used consistently by Matthew with prophecy. He describes an event taking place **that it might be fulfilled which was spoken by the prophets** (Matthew 2:23). Here the idea is one of completion or being filled to the brim. The recorded event has been placed into the prophecy and fills this container full with the proper content.

This is the impact of Luke's statement in our passage. ***And suddenly there came a sound from heaven, as of a rushing mighty wind, and it filled the whole house where they were sitting*** (Acts 2:2). In the grammar structure of the sentence there is no choice but to relate the filling with the ***sound.*** This is more startling than it may appear upon the first reading. If there had been an actual tempest, it would have been frightening. If there had been a blasting, furious wind, there would have been destruction. But this would have been understandable because such storms often happened. But there was no storm, no wind, no rain, nor thunder. The entire attention of the disciples was focused on the *sound*. Visible objects looking like *divided tongues* (Acts 2:3) came upon each person. They appeared as fire, but there was no fire. Thus, the descent of the Holy Spirit was not only heard but also seen. The initial descent of the Holy Spirit ushers in the life of the Kingdom of God.

Jesus described this to His disciples as being *baptized with the Holy Spirit* (Acts 1:5). Peter was present at the Jerusalem Council when the issue of the Gentiles and Christianity was discussed. Peter related his personal involvement in the outpouring of the Holy Spirit upon the Gentiles. He said, *"And as I began to speak, the Holy Spirit fell upon them, as upon us at the beginning. Then I remembered the word of the Lord, how He said, 'John indeed baptized with water, but you shall be baptized with the Holy Spirit,'"* (Acts 11:15-16).

The concept of *baptized* was not new to the disciples or the Jewish culture. There is a strong distinction between the root Greek word (bapto) and the expanded Greek word for *baptized* (baptidzo). The basic idea is to dip repeatedly, to immerse or submerge. However, to illustrate the difference between the two words, the Greek lexicons give a recipe for making pickles. In order to make a pickle, the vegetable should first be dipped (bapto) into boiling water and then *baptized* (baptidzo) in the vinegar solution. Both verbs involve immersing the vegetable. But the first (bapto) is temporary while the second (baptidzo) produces a permanent change.

This is the reality of Luke's intent in verses two and three. This was the initial baptism of the Holy Spirit upon the believers. It brought about a permanent change in the structure of the Kingdom of God as well as in the lives of individual believers. It is the official announcement of the shift from the old covenant to the new covenant. God is no longer going to walk with man; He is going to walk in man! A permanent change takes place in how God is going to relate to mankind. The church is born!

However, this is not only true in a general, corporate sense, but also on the individual basis. Each individual believer received his own personal baptism of the Holy Spirit. Luke describes this as *and one sat upon each of them* (Acts 2:3). Paul discovered some disciples in Ephesus. He inquired of them, *"Did you receive the Holy Spirit when you believed?"* (Acts 19:2). They answered that they had not even as much as heard of the Holy Spirit. Paul continued to question them. He asked, *"Into what then were you baptized?" So they said, "Into John's baptism,"* (Acts 19:3). He immediately led them into a baptism in the name of the Lord Jesus, *and when Paul had laid hands on them, the Holy Spirit came upon them* (Acts 19:6). Paul expressed this by writing, *for by one Spirit we were all baptized into one body — whether Jews or Greeks, whether slaves or free — and have all been made to drink into one Spirit* (1 Corinthians 12:13). A permanent change (not meaning eternal security) has taken place in the individual life of a believer through this baptism.

Again Luke describes this as, *and suddenly there came a sound from heaven, as of a rushing mighty wind, and it filled the whole house where they were sitting* (Acts 2:2). This filling of the Holy Spirit expressed in the verse relates to the baptism of the Holy Spirit. It has to do with that which was outside coming to be inside. What an overwhelming experience it is to be filled with the Spirit of Jesus in a moment of time. There is no salvation outside of the infilling. We find a permanent change (baptidzo) in the embrace of this Person.

It is important to note the Greek word for *filled* in this verse is in the active voice. The subject is responsible for the action of the filling. It is the *sound* (Spirit of Jesus) who is responsible for the infilling during this baptism of the Holy Spirit. There is absolutely no self-effort that contributes to this. We have done nothing to accomplish this. If God ever comes to live within us, it will be exclusively a result of His action toward us. Will we allow Him to act upon us?

This brings us to the second major Greek word for *filled* (Acts 2:4). It gives us something of a contrasting picture to that described in the previous paragraphs. ***And they were all filled with the Holy Spirit and began to speak with other tongues, as the spirit gave them utterance*** (Acts 2:4). The Greek word Luke uses in this verse is distinctly different from the word in verse two. In verse two the idea expressed is that something outside was coming inside. The focus was on "to fill with content." However, now Luke shifts to a Greek word which focuses on the content which is already present coming to an end or permeating the whole. It is used to describe what takes place in a sponge. ***Immediately one of them ran and took a sponge, filled it with sour wine and put it on a reed, and offered it to Him to drink*** (Matthew 27:48). This presents the concept of saturation, soaking, flow, or permeating.

The Greek word for *filled* implies a purposed plan which is now coming to an end. The gift of languages in this passage did not come to the disciples. It was the Holy Spirit who was already within them who began to flow in this method of ministry. This was an expression of the already present Spirit of Christ who was permeating their lives to accomplish and fill up this new purpose of proclamation. Another example of this is found in the life of Peter. He, along with others, has been put in jail for the night. They are being interrogated by the leaders of Israel. Something takes place in his life as he addresses the group. ***Then Peter, filled with the Holy Spirit, said to them, "Rulers of the people and elders of Israel:"*** (Acts 4:8). Luke is not saying that the Spirit of preaching came and filled Peter for this occasion. This is not something outside of him that came to be inside. Peter had already received the Holy Spirit who now began to fill him with the ability to minister in this method.

It must be understood this is the Greek word which is consistently connected to the movement of the Holy Spirit in the disciples throughout the Book of Acts. What a picture this paints for us! God wants to actually come to be within us. We are to be the temple of the Holy Spirit. It is in this receiving of the Spirit of Christ (baptism) that the most intimate relationship is established. The Holy Spirit is then on a moment by moment basis filling the purpose He wants to accomplish. We become an instrument of the expression of the Spirit of Jesus! He has a plan; we are the means by which He is filling that plan to completion.

What would happen if you saw the circumstances of your life from this view? Look at Peter again. He has just been used to bring five thousand men into the Kingdom of God (Acts 4:4). What should be an occasion of great joy became a circumstance of great pressure. The leaders of Israel are offended and order the capture of those involved in this evangelistic endeavor. It is evening when they are taken into custody. This required that they spend the night in jail before having a proper hearing. Think of how you would feel if this happened to you. You tried to do the right thing and it has become a tragic mess! You know what these very same leaders of Israel are capable of doing when threatened. They are the ones who crucified Christ. What should you do? How should you respond? Peter is our example. He relaxed in the Spirit of God who had come to be within him. He refused to own the situation as his. He allowed the Spirit of Christ to fill his circumstance. Peter realized the Holy Spirit had a purposed plan and would fill that plan with the accomplished end by His power.

This is exactly the situation in our passage (Acts 2:4). The disciples have received the Holy Spirit (Acts 2:2). No doubt they are in the temple at this time. They spend most of their time during this waiting period in the temple. They are rejoicing and praising God over what He has done in the resurrection and what He is going to do in the days ahead. This is where the large crowd has gathered (Acts 2:9-11). The Spirit of Christ has an agenda. He could simply fill the one hundred and twenty disciples and later make plans for church planting. However, there is a multitude to which com-munication of truth is needed. The disciples who receive the Holy Spirit now are instruments through which the Spirit can accomplish His purposed plan. He fills them, brings His immediate purpose to a completion as they speak in languages they do not know. This is not the outside Spirit of tongues which comes to be inside of them, but the Holy Spirit who is already indwelling them permeating their lives to fill up His purposed plan!

The Book of Acts demonstrates the very essence of Christian living. Do you grasp the consistent, moment by moment surrender to the control of the Spirit of Christ this requires? The very baptism of the Holy Spirit requires a dying which must continue. This is not just an experience to remember, but a life to be lived. The depth of surrender, the crucifixion achieved in the fullness of the Spirit of Christ must be maintained in living or all is lost. The dream of God was not just to give you His life, but to manifest His life through you in every circumstance. It is a "filling," to bring to an end His accomplished purpose. This is a call to a "living dying."

There is one other major idea which is connected to this Greek word *filled.* In the Greek language, the basic root word used in *they were all filled* is sometimes used with the prefix "in." It means "to fill" therefore "to satisfy." In a sermon preached in Lystra, Barnabas and Paul defend the greatness of God. The people thought they were gods who had come down to earth. Barnabas and Paul declared, **"Nevertheless He did not leave Himself without witness, in that He did good, gave us rain from heaven and fruitful seasons, filling our hearts with food and gladness,"** (Acts 14:17). It is a testimony that God has indeed satisfied our desires. It is interesting that this Greek word is used only in relation to food. It is used in the story of the feeding of the five thousand. **So when they were filled, He said to His disciples, "Gather up the fragments that remain, so that nothing is lost,"** (John 6:12). However, this Greek word is never used in connection with the filling of the Holy Spirit.

The emphasis of the fullness of the Holy Spirit is not on being completed in terms of satisfaction, enough, ended or finished. There is a continual flow to the movement of the Spirit of God. The picture of the filling of the Holy Spirit is not the gluttonous, satisfied, holding his belling, eating too much, overweight, overfed and spoiled Christian. It is the picture of the Christian on the edge of his seat anticipating the action of the Holy Spirit who is already with him. What will the Spirit of Christ do through me in the midst of this crisis? What attitudes will the Spirit of Christ flow through me?

This is so strongly emphasized in the New Testament that the satisfied, gluttonous, holding his belly Christian is viewed as not experiencing the filling of the Holy Spirit. It is a contradiction in terms. It simply cannot be! There is no filling of the Holy Spirit for satisfaction. Other words which bespeak this same condition might be; comfortable, arrival, finished, ingrown and completed. The filling of the Holy Spirit is characterized by such words as: seeking, expecting, desiring, hungering, thirsting, yielding, surrendering, depending and openness.

The purpose of the baptism of the Spirit of Christ is the filling of the Spirit of Christ. Christ comes to live within us for the purpose of flowing through us to accomplish a purposed plan. This is the sourcing of the Spirit which Jesus proposed to His disciples. ***"But you shall receive power when the Holy Spirit has come upon you; and you shall be witnesses to Me in Jerusalem, and in Judea and Samaria, and to the end of the earth,"*** (Acts 1:8). The baptism of the Holy Spirit was to bring to death all self-sourcing. As Jesus constantly lived in the filling of the Father, so we are to constantly live in the filling of the Spirit of Christ. As Jesus was consistently sourced by the Father, so we are to be sourced by the Spirit of Christ. Think of the life that could be lived in the power and sourcing of God! It would be the Christ life!

6

TO BE SEATED

ACTS 2:3

In verse one, Luke pin-points the exact time the Promise of the Father was fulfilled. It was on the Day of the Feast of Pentecost. It marked the fulfillment of the dreams of God to restore us to the full purpose for which He made us. We have again become the container of the Spirit of God. He has come! In verse two, Luke attempts to discuss the wonder of this coming. There was a sound (echo) which was like a great and mighty wind. The disciples heard this. There was also that which they saw in verse three. It was like a tongue appearing as fire. It separated and came upon each one of the believers individually. The process is described as **sat upon each of them** (Acts 2:3).

The Greek word translated *sat* is most unique. It is used forty-eight times in the New Testament, but it always has a particular slant or tone to it. One must realize that the author had a multitude of choices. There were numerous words available to describe the coming of this object which looked like a tongue of fire. He might have used a word which would have stated the Holy Spirit was "coming upon" the disciples. If he wanted to emphasize the permanent remaining of the Holy Spirit upon the believers, he could have used the Greek word meaning "resting upon." Even if his desire was to simply tell us that the Holy Spirit "sat" upon the disciples, the normal Greek word for "sat" could have been used.

However, Luke chose a Greek word which is uniquely used for authority. This Greek word is used exclusively for someone sitting down in the place of authority. A King does not simply sit down; he does whatever this word projects! Let me give you some examples of the usage of this Greek word. After choosing His disciples, Jesus went to a mountain and "sat down" to proclaim the manifesto of the Kingdom of God in the Sermon on the Mount (Matthew 5:1). Two disciples who were brothers enlisted their mother in a request. They wanted the right and left hand positions in the coming Kingdom of God. The word used throughout the passage to describe their achieving these positions is this Greek word (Matthew 20:21). Jesus is preaching His final public message to the multitude. In describing the scribes and the Pharisees, He says, **"The scribes and the Pharisees SIT in Moses' seat,"** (Matthew 23:2). This was the place of authority when one spoke the Law of God. Paul was on trial and found himself before Festus. Festus was intrigued with Paul, **and the next day, SITTING on the judgment seat, he commanded Paul to be brought** (Acts 25:6).

It is amazing the number of times this word is used in the Book of Acts. Luke highlights this word nine times. We just referred to one of them. He also writes, **So on a set day Herod, arrayed in royal apparel, SAT** *on his throne and gave an oration to them* (Acts 12:21). In Peter's sermon on Pentecost Day, he reminded them of the promise God made to King David. He said, **"Therefore, being a prophet and knowing that God had sworn with an oath to him that of the fruit of his body, according to the flesh, He would raise up the Christ to SIT on his throne,"** (Acts 2:30).

This word is used consistently to describe the enthroning of Jesus as King of the Kingdom. Matthew quotes Jesus as saying, **"Assuredly I say to you, that in the regeneration, when the Son of Man SITS on the throne of His glory, you who have followed Me will also SIT on twelve thrones, judging the twelve tribes of Israel,"** (Matthew 19:28). Paul describes the great power of God **which He worked in Christ when He raised Him from the dead and SEATED Him at His right hand in the heavenly places** (Ephesians 1:20). The writer of the Book of Hebrews uses this word several times to express the authority of Christ. In describing Jesus, he writes, **who being the brightness of His glory and the express image of His person, and upholding all things by the word of His power, when He had by Himself purged our sins, SAT down at the right hand of the Majesty on high** (Hebrews 1:3). In summarizing the first seven chapters, he says, **Now this is the main point of the things we are saying: We have such a High Priest, who is SEATED at the right hand of the throne of the Majesty in the heavens,** (Hebrews 8:1). He contrasted the greatness of the sacrifice of Christ with the Old Testament sacrifices. **But this Man, after He had offered one sacrifice for sins forever, SAT down at the right hand of God** (Hebrews 10:12). The promises of Christ spill forth from the Book of Revelation. The ascended Lord promises ***"To him who overcomes I will grant to SIT with Me on My throne, as I also overcame and SAT down with My Father on His throne,"*** (Revelation 3:21). John saw something overwhelming in the future of the saints. ***And I saw thrones, and they SAT on them, and judgment was committed to them. Then I saw the souls of those who had been beheaded for their witness to Jesus and for the word of God, who had not worshiped the beast or his image, and had not received his mark on their foreheads or on their hands. And they lived and reigned with Christ for a thousand years*** (Revelation 20:4).

If you have grasped the tone of this great word, I would like to suggest a radical concept. Dare we take for granted the use of this Greek word in relation to the Day of Pentecost? As this word is forcibly used to describe the enthroning of Christ, it is now used to describe the enthroning of the Holy Spirit in our lives. As the word depicts who Jesus is as King of the Kingdom, now it depicts who the Holy Spirit is within us. What is happening in the heavenly realms is in like manner taking place in the earthly realms. Christ enthroned at the right hand of the Father as King of the Kingdom is parallel to the Spirit of Jesus now enthroned as King of the Kingdom within you!

Would this not be the complete fulfillment of the prayer of Jesus?

"In this manner, therefore pray:
Our Father in heaven,
Hallowed be Your name.
Your kingdom come,
Your will be done
On earth as it is in heaven," (Matthew 6:9-10).

Jesus gives us pointed teaching about this concept. He began to use "church" language with His disciples. He describes the church and a group of people who have linked with what is taking place in heaven (Matthew 18:18). In turn they have reached out to link with each other (Matthew 18:19). With one arm embracing all that is in heaven and one arm embracing each other there begins to be a flow from heaven to earth. In this connection and flow the image of Christ is produced in their world (Matthew 18:20). What a progression this is! The foundation of it all is linking with heaven. What is happening there must begin to happen here within us.

Again, consider carefully this truth! Is the Day of Pentecost, the outpouring of the Holy Spirit upon the believers, a duplication of what is taking place in the ascension of Christ? As Christ ascended to the heavenly realm and was seated at the right hand of the Father, did the Spirit of Jesus descend to the earthly realm and "sit" upon the believer? Is this what the fullness of the Holy Spirit is?

I must confess this is a change in focus and emphasis regarding the baptism of the Holy Spirit. Perhaps the real focus of the Holy Spirit is not about empowering but about reigning. Perhaps His real purpose is not about miracles, but about ruling. The Biblical concept of the Kingdom of God is completely opposite from the concept of the kingdom of the world. In our world, we consider a kingdom in terms of space, acres, population, budgets, power, size, etc., and in the Bible the Kingdom of God is always about God reigning. Where ever God reigns, there is the Kingdom! In answering the Pharisees, Jesus said, **"The kingdom of God does not come with observation;**

nor will they say, 'See here!' or 'See there!' For indeed, the kingdom of God is within you," (Luke 17:20-21). If the Kingdom of God is within us, it requires the presence and reigning of the King. Is the fullness of the Holy Spirit in the life of the believer the coronation of Christ as King of the Kingdom of God? The Spirit of Christ is SITTING on His throne here in the exact same manner that Christ is SITTING on His throne there!

While this may all sound great theologically, what does it mean in practical life experience? This is what really matters to most of us. How does this affect my life on a daily basis? We must come back to the text. ***Then there appeared to them divided tongues, as of fire, and one sat upon each of them*** (Acts 2:3). The Greek word which is translated ***divided*** is actually a verb in the form of a participle. In this case it acts like an adjective modifying the word ***tongues.*** The emphasis of the word is on separation (to separate into parts or divide up). It gives you the idea that the tongues were divided out to each person from one common source. This gives you the picture of a fire-like appearance coming into the room corresponding with the hearing of the sound. At first it appeared as a single unit, but suddenly it parted in every direction. A portion of it ***sat*** on each of those who were present.

The Greek word translated ***tongues*** is definitely plural. The passive, participle ***divided*** gives a description of what happens with these ***tongues.*** They were together as if a whole unit, but then began to divide. The Greek word translated ***sat*** describes what happens to each person. The outpouring of the Holy Spirit was upon each person individually. It is a personal experience. The Holy Spirit *sat* upon each individual disciple! Does God want to do this in my life?

However, to grasp the significance of this we must see it through the understanding of the word *sat*. The Spirit of Christ is coming to SIT upon the individual believer in the same way the ascended Lord went to SIT at the right hand of the Father. We must see the outpouring of the Holy Spirit in light of this parallel. The emphasis is not upon the Spirit of Christ reigning over you. This is not the Holy Spirit coming to be your King. He did not come to indwell us so He could be our boss. In light of the word *sat* we must see that He has come in order to reign FROM us not over us. We are the actual platform of His authority.

Picture with me the heavenly realm and the great throne of God, the Father. At His right hand is the throne of authority which belongs to the King of the Kingdom. It belongs to the one to whom the Father gives it. At the base of the mountain, the resurrected Lord said to His disciples. **"All authority has been given to Me in heaven and on earth,"** (Matthew 28:18). What does this throne look like? Is it gold plated? Do not let your focus be on the physical aspect (if there actually is one) of the throne. Let your attention be upon the throne as the platform from which He reigns. Now transfer that picture into the descending of the Holy Spirit who has come to sit upon you as a believer! You are the throne which has nothing to do with shape or gold, but platform for authority. Your life is to be the throne from which the authority of the Spirit of Christ, who is the King of the Kingdom is distributed. He is not just reigning over you but from you!

One scholar says this about the Greek word translated *sat*. "In the New Testament this highest human concept is used to express the inexpressible." This tells you the dilemma in which we find ourselves. What is the difference between Christ reigning OVER us and reigning FROM us? I am afraid the difference is inexpressible! But do we not have to attempt to grasp the great concept?

When He reigns OVER us, we are told what to do and are expected to be obedient. However, when He reigns FROM us, we become an avenue through which He demonstrates His Kingship and authority. We will most likely be totally unaware of what He is accomplishing. But the authority of Christ is accomplishing a great plan! When He reigns OVER us, we must discipline ourselves to come under His authority. Spiritual disciplines are necessary to bend our rebellious tendencies to His purposes. When He reigns FROM us, we find self-control as a fruit of the Spirit (Galatians 5:22-23). What we are experiencing is completely beyond self-contribution. When He reigns OVER us, we find ourselves obligated because He has done so much for us. When He reigns FROM us, we experience the thrill of being a part of the very heart of God being displayed in our world.

Surely you must recognize this is far beyond and on a higher plane than surrender. All my life I have heard "total surrender" taught and preached. I have sung the favorite song, "I Surrender All." Total surrender is always focused on things or items. I am never sure I have surrendered everything to Christ because I am always finding new things or areas of my life which I have not faced. Christ is constantly revealing new aspects of His greatness which I have not experienced. These may be areas of which I am not aware. When these things are revealed I must surrender them. I wonder if I am capable of surrendering all things to Christ. The conclusion is I must continually surrender everything to Christ. It is going to be a life time experience of always surrendering.

When He comes to reign FROM me, I am moved to another realm. This is far beyond surrender. Every aspect of my life becomes a platform upon which He can display Himself to my world. I become a dispenser from which He distributes His authority and power. I am the stage upon which He manifests His greatness. It is the fulfillment of Paul's statement, **But we have this treasure in earthen vessels, that the excellence of the power may be of God and not of us** (2 Corinthians 4:7). The **earthen vessel** is the clay "cracked" flower pot. Its total purpose of existence is to contain something. The beauty of the flower it holds so masters the viewer that the clay pot is unnoticed. God has designed us to be used like the clay pot. Our purpose is **that the excellence of the power may be of God and not of us.** He is reigning FROM us.

It is amazing to embrace this concept and read the Book of Acts with this distinction. One hundred and twenty individuals have just received the Spirit of Christ reigning FROM them. They are in a crowded place where at least seventeen different nationalities and languages are represented. Suddenly the Gospel message is being proclaimed in each of these languages. The crowd is confused. They are not confused with the message but the deliverance of the message. How can these uneducated Galileans know all of these languages? This does not have anything to do with these unlearned Galileans. They have become a platform upon which the dynamic of the Spirit of Christ is reigning. The Truth (Christ is the Truth) must be communicated. It is definitely the fulfillment of the promise that they will become His witnesses. Therefore, witnessing must be defined as the demonstration of the authority of Christ reigning FROM the believer without the contribution of his knowledge, skill, or talent. It is not the product of seminars or training. It is Him reigning from the believer.

You and I need to radically apply this to our lives. It appears that the average evangelical believer of this generation has a Christianity which he has mastered. Perhaps he has received some kind of touch from God, but has proceeded to live his life as a product of his training. Even in our discipleship programs we are strong on the emphasis of developing our Christian patterns. We develop follow-up material which teaches the new convert to do the right things and have the right disciplines. Do you understand how far beneath Christ ruling FROM us this is? Have we developed a Christianity which is a product of ourselves? We reap meager results and have little affect on our world. We spend our time developing programs. We busy ourselves with our buildings and maintenance. But the action of the Holy Spirit as in the Book of Acts is missing. We allow the Spirit of Christ to reign OVER us. He dictates our actions and practices. No one can accuse us of being unchristian in deed or word. But the Holy Spirit reigning FROM us is missing.

Do I need the sound of His presence to come again? Do I need what looks like a tongue of fire to separate itself and come and *sit* on me?

7
FILLED WITH WHAT?
ACTS 2:4

Luke confronts us repeatedly with the reality of the "fullness of the Holy Spirit" in the Book of Acts. This is not a minor issue that can be easily dismissed. This is the central focus of the book and all the historical information concerning the spread of the church is a testimony to it. To miss this would be to miss it all!

We must restate the distinction of this book. It is the baptism of the Spirit and the filling of the Spirit. This distinction is found in the contrast between the two Greek words translated *filled* in verses two and four (Acts 2:2,4). In verse two, the Greek word refers to content which is placed in a container. It is something outside coming inside. The Holy Spirit, both heard in the sound and seen in the tongue as of fire, has come! While He was present in Old Testament days, He has now come to fill the container in a new way. It is both a corporate and individual filling. The Church was born in the initial outpouring of the

Promise of the Father. But the tongues as of fire separated and rested on each individual believer (Acts 2:3). Each person experienced this baptism of the Holy Spirit. Paul describes it as ***for by one Spirit we were all baptized into one body — whether Jews or Greeks, whether slaves or free — and have all been made to drink into one Spirit*** (1 Corinthians 12:13).

In verse four the Greek word translated ***filled*** describes a flow of something which is already present. It is not outside coming inside, but inside permeating and saturating. The baptism of the Holy Spirit is equaled with initial sanctification. It is the new birth! The very life of Christ has come to be within the believer. Justification (forgiveness) has taken place and the believer has been invaded by the Spirit of Christ. The fullness of the Holy Spirit is equated with entire sanctification. It is not something different, but a continuation of what has already happened. The Holy Spirit already present within moves to fill the entire being. This requires crucifixion of self-will. The carnal mind must be put to death.

In the baptism of the Spirit, I belong to His body (1 Corinthians 12:13). The fullness of the Spirit means that my body now belongs to Him. The baptism of the Spirit of Christ does not need to take place again. The fullness of the Spirit of Christ is repeated again and again as I die daily to the patterns of my established self-will. The Holy Spirit will constantly fill me in new demonstrations of His being. I will grow in the embrace of Christ. The baptism of the Holy Spirit links me with other believers (Ephesians 4:1-6). The fullness of the Spirit is personal and individual.

Paul commands us to be filled with the Spirit. ***And do***

not be drunk with wine, in which is dissipation; but be filled with the Spirit (Ephesians 5:18). The grammar of this verb be *filled* is the present, passive, imperative. This indicates that the Spirit is to be continuously filling the believer. Paul then begins to list the results of being filled with the Spirit (Ephesians 5:19-33). He restates this list in the Book of Colossians (3:16-25), and he says these things are a result of having a mind saturated with the Word of God! He says, *"Let the word of Christ dwell in you richly,"* (Colossians 3:16). To let the Word of Christ richly dwell in you is identical to being filled with the Spirit. These two are the same spiritual reality viewed from two sides. To be filled with the Spirit is to be controlled by His Word. To have the Word dwelling richly in you is to be controlled by His Spirit. Since the Holy Spirit is the author and the power of the Word, the expressions are interchangeable. Therefore, Paul gives the same results for each one!

Let us examine these two parallel statements: ***Let the word of Christ dwell in you richly*** (Colossians 3:16). ***But be filled with the Spirit*** (Ephesians 5:18). Is there a difference between ***dwell in you richly*** and ***be filled?*** The Greek word translated ***dwell*** means to dwell within, live in or among. It is fascinating to contrast the use of this Greek word in the Greek translation of the Old Testament (Septuagint) and the Greek New Testament. It is used in the Septuagint for human dwelling and settling on earth. This takes place in the land, on mountains, or in cities. This Greek word is used to refer to the human possession of these places. Thus, this word becomes a fixed term for "inhabitants." God is never the subject of this Greek word. In the Old Testament, man is constantly indwelling (land, mountains, cities, etc.) but God never indwells. In the

Old Testament God is never an inhabitant!

In the New Testament it is completely the opposite. Mankind is never the subject of this word. Man becomes the object or the dwelling place. Man is indwelt by sin. Paul stated it, ***But now, it is no longer I who do it, but sin that dwells in me*** (Romans 7:17). Mankind can definitely be indwelt by the Holy Spirit. Again Paul states, ***that good thing which was committed to you, keep by the Holy Spirit who dwells in us*** (2 Timothy 1:14). Another way of saying this is that God indwells you. Paul said, ***and what agreement has the temple of God with idols? For you are the temple of the living God. As God has said:***

"I will dwell in them
And walk among them.
I will be their God,
And they shall be my people," (2 Corinthians 6:16).

Human beings can even be indwelt by faith. Paul wrote, ***When I call to remembrance the genuine faith that is in you, which dwelt first in your grandmother Lois and your mother Eunice, and I am persuaded is in you also*** (2 Timothy 1:5). In the same manner man can be indwelt by God's Word. ***Let the Word of God dwell in you richly*** (Colossians 3:16).

A shift is made between the Old and New Testament. Man has moved from being the inhabitant to being the habitat. The New Testament view is that an individual is actually indwelt by an external Being of power. This Being actually comes within the human being to live. This Being is able to dominate that individual. The person's body becomes a "house" or "temple" of this Being. Obviously there are only two possibilities by which a person can be indwelt. There is God and the devil. Romans chapter seven would convince us that the devil continuously takes possession of a person, dominates that person, and has him or her in his power. Sin not only controls the actions of the person (Romans 7:7) but also acts in place of that person (Romans 7:18). It forces the person to do what he or she does not want to do and drives the person to destruction.

The opposite picture of this is a person being indwelt by the Spirit of Christ. It is only the Spirit of Christ who can break the power of the one who has possessed us. Paul cries out, ***But if the Spirit of Him who raised Jesus from the dead dwells in you, He who raised Christ from the dead will also give life to your mortal bodies through the Spirit who dwells in you*** (Romans 8:11). We are considering the passage in Colossians. ***Let the word of Christ dwell in you richly*** (Colossians 3:16). Paul states this in the imperative; so this is a command. We are ordered to allow the Word of Christ to be at home in us ***richly.*** This Greek word can also be translated abundantly or extravagantly rich. In this verse, the word can be used in two ways. It can be an adjective of the ***word of Christ.*** Who could possibly dispute the richness, abundance, and extravagant wealth of the Scriptures? Who can dismiss the Gospel account and the depth of the movement of God in our behalf as if it is a cheap issue? The ***word of Christ*** must be taken in the full expanse of its abundance. However, this word ***richly*** can also apply to how the ***word of Christ*** indwells the believer. Every area of the believer's life must be dominated and richly possessed by the Word. This is not one aspect or ingredient within him; this is the abundance, the completeness of the indwelling.

Now, how does this compare with the use of the word *filled?* In Ephesians (5:18) the believer is commanded (imperative) to *be filled with the Spirit!* The Greek word which is translated *filled* is the same as Luke's description of the sound filling the whole house (Acts 2:2). It has the idea of something outside coming to be inside, but it definitely has completeness about it. The concept of abundantly, extrav-agantly rich is engrained within the word. There is no difference between the "filling" and the "indwelling."

Let us now consider the comparison of *the Spirit* and *the word of Christ.* Is there a difference? Obviously *the Spirit* is a reference to the Holy Spirit who came in an outpouring on the Day of Pentecost (Acts 2:1-4). The Holy Spirit is not an "it" but a person! He is so closely linked and united with Christ that we refer to Him as the Spirit of Christ. To be *filled* with the Holy Spirit is to be filled with Christ. Paul refers to being *filled with the Spirit* (Ephesians 5:18) and *Christ in you* (Colossians 1:27). In the upper room before His death, Jesus spent time relating the promise of the Father to His disciples. He said, *"And I will pray the Father, and He will give you another Helper, that He may abide with you forever — the Spirit of truth, whom the world cannot receive, because it neither sees Him nor knows Him; but you know Him, for He dwells with you and will be in you. I will not leave you orphans; I will come to you,"* (John 14:16-18). Jesus refers to the Holy Spirit with you as Himself!

The Biblical concept of *the word of Christ* is never a story narrative, doctrinal statement, or theology. *The word of Christ* is always linked with the person of Christ. It is impossible to separate them. While the communication may come from Christ, the communication is always considered Christ. This is why Jesus could say, *"I am the way, the truth, and the life,"* (John 14:6). The Living Word is speaking the Written Word. It is an extension of His very being and is considered Him. It is impossible for His Word to be other than He is!

God gives us a tremendous opportunity in the Gospel. He calls us to the rich, full and complete filling of His Person within our very beings. This very Person speaks to us in His Word. He is not writing it down and later we are to study it on our own. No! The interaction of the Word in our lives is God Himself speaking His Word to us as we saturate in it. Is this not a call to saturate, feed upon, live in and completely immerse ourselves in the Scriptures, His Word? The fullness of His Spirit requires the saturation in His Word. Saturation in His Word requires the fullness of His Spirit. No wonder the Apostle Paul says they are the same.

Here are two statements which are so interlocked that to say one is to speak the other. They are the same. **Let the word of Christ dwell in you richly** (Colossians 3:16). **But be filled with the Spirit** (Ephesians 5:18). From these two (same) statements Paul gives a list of results. The list is virtually the same for both. It contains three strong elements which are fundamental to all of Christian experience; they hardly need to be explained. What does need explanation is their focus! These three elements must not be seen as the cause, only as the result. One does not do these three things and then have the fullness of the Holy Spirit and the Word of Christ indwelt. These are the natural byproduct of the presence of Christ. To state it stronger — these are always present when the Holy Spirit is filling the individual.

SINGING

Paul says we are to be *speaking to one another in psalms and hymns and spiritual songs, singing and making melody in your heart to the Lord* (Ephesians 5:19). This is a result of being filled with the Spirit. He also says, *Let the word of Christ dwell in you richly in all wisdom, teaching and admonishing one another in psalms and hymns and spiritual songs, singing with grace in your hearts to the Lord* (Colossians 3:16). These are very specific statements. Notice the idea of *psalms and hymns and spiritual songs* in both passages. The content of the singing is a total focus on the Word of Christ. From a Biblical view there is no song outside of this content. I am not sure what this does to secular music, but it is a fake, fraud, and an attempt to duplicate the greatness of our God. The song is not to be an expression of personal feelings or experiences but a *word of Christ.* If the preacher is obligated to base his sermon on Scripture, how much more the singer! If every sermon is to be an explanation and exposing of the Scripture, how much more the song! Therefore the basis of worship is always the Word. The melody, beat, and rhythm is unimportant to the worshipper. The reason the believer can worship is because of the truth. Style of worship becomes insignificant. It is the expression of truth which inspires worship within the believer.

Both of Paul's statements contain a focus on *in your heart.* One dare not say, "I am not a musical person. I have no musical ability and therefore do not sing." What about the music produced by the Holy Spirit within you? The expression of it may be quite sad, but it must be expressed. The **heart** is the seat of all life. If there is music in the heart, how can it not be expressed? Should it not be on your face, in your eyes, and dominate your talk?

SUPPER OF THE LORD

Paul continues by saying, we are ***giving thanks always for all things to God the Father in the name of our Lord Jesus Christ,*** (Ephesians 5:20). In his parallel passage he says, ***And whatever you do in word or deed, do all in the name of the Lord Jesus, giving thanks to God the Father through Him*** (Colossians 3:17). Do you see the strong parallel between ***for all things*** and ***do all?*** There is something all inclusive in these statements. This powerful gratitude within the believer affects everything!

How can Paul be so bold as to make such a broad statement? The Greek word for ***giving thanks*** is the same root word for Eucharist. All of life is an act of coming to the table of our Lord. Remember our study of the Day of the Feast of Pentecost. They called it the "concluding assembly of the Passover." It was the celebration of the conclusion of the harvest. Israel saw the harvest as a result of the Passover, the blood of the lamb. The reason they had the land, established a home, had a family, and planted a crop was because of the lamb. If everything is seen in light of the blood of Christ, would we not live in constant gratitude? Where do griping, complaining, and dismay fit into this?

SUBMIT

Paul continues, ***submitting to one another in the fear of God*** (Ephesians 5:20). In his parallel passage he says, ***Wives, submit…*** (Colossians 3:18); ***Husbands, love…*** (Colossians 3:19); ***Children, obey…*** (Colossians 3:20); ***Bondservants, obey…*** (Colossians 3:22); ***And whatever you do, do it heartily, as to the Lord and not to men*** (Colossians 3:23). It is very significant that the material in both passages on this subject is lengthy. Perhaps it is here that we have our major problem. He seems compelled to give illustrations and break it down into our every day relationships.

It must be recognized that submission is not an "act" but an "attitude." It is a spontaneous result of being filled with the Spirit of the Word. It does not come from obligation. It is not the result of power, fear, or intimidation. It is the natural flow of the Spirit of Jesus.

These three elements are results not criteria for being filled with the Sprit of God. One does not do these things and then become filled with the Spirit and indwelt by the Word. It is because the Word richly indwells the believer that these three things happen. If they are not present, it is an immediate warning for concern. Their absence tells us of our lack. Examine your life through the eyes of Christ.

8

THE SPIRIT'S MOUTHPIECE
ACTS 2:4

The Word of God has much to say about the tongue. The tongue is described as wicked, deceitful, perverse, filthy, corrupt, flattering, slanderous, gossiping, blasphemous, foolish, boasting, complaining, cursing, contentious, sensual, and vile. No wonder God put the tongue in a cage behind the teeth, walled in by the mouth! Someone observed that because the tongue is in a wet place, it can easily slip.

Some sins are not committed because there isn't an opportunity. However, the tongue is always available, ready, and anxious. There are no limits or built-in restraints. Scientists propose that once a sound wave produced by the tongue is set in motion, it continues on a never-ending journey. If we had sophisticated enough instruments, each wave could be captured and reproduced at any time. This would mean that every word spoken by any person who has ever lived could be retrieved!

Could that be the judgment day review? God simply does a replay of every word you and I have spoken. We judge ourselves by our own tongue. No wonder Jesus said, **"For by your words you will be justified, and by your words you will be condemned,"** (Matthew 12:37).

James writes very pointedly about this issue in his epistle. He mentions the tongue in every chapter of his epistle (James 1:19, 26; 2:12; 3:5, 6, 8; 4:11; 5:12). He describes the controlling power of the tongue with various illustrations. ***Indeed, we put bits in horses' mouths that they may obey us, and we turn their whole body*** (James 3:3). His analogy is strong. So our entire life or body will be controlled by our tongue. He goes on to speak of large sail boats which are controlled by a small rudder (James 3:4). The tongue is the rudder of our life determining the direction in which we go. The tongue is an indicator of a person's spirit; it reveals what is in the heart!

Do you not find it fascinating that Luke describes the first expression of the filling of the Holy Spirit as that of the tongue! Those filled with the Spirit become the Spirit's mouthpiece. In the language of James, the Spirit of Jesus has harnessed the very heart of the believer's life. He has taken control of the rudder of man's ship. However, Luke takes this concept one step further. The Holy Spirit does not just control what is being said, He is actually saying it. The Holy Spirit does not tell the believer His message and the believer delivers it. This implies separation from the Holy Spirit. There is a merging of the life of the Spirit and the believer. The mind of the Spirit becomes the mind of the believer. The believer's tongue now becomes the Spirit's tongue!

In studying our passage (Acts 2:4) we will begin with the conclusion and then work through the passage to be sure it is verified. The Spirit of Jesus desires to permeate our faculties in order to produce through our tongue His message to our world. He is not asking us to speak in His behalf. He wants to speak through us. He is not holding seminars for our training in proper spiritual communication. He is merging with the believer in an intimate union which will produce one mind, one voice, and one message! Now let us view the passage.

The opening statement of verse four is ***They were all filled with the Holy Spirit*** (Acts 2:4). One Biblical scholar states, "To be filled with anything is a phrase denoting that all the faculties are pervaded by it, engaged in it, or under its influence." Let your mind grasp the reality of such an invasion of the Spirit of Christ in your life. Remember the emphasis of the Greek word translated *filled* in this verse (Acts 2:4). It is contrasted with a different Greek word translated *filled* in verse two. Verse two refers to content actually coming into a container. It is the picture of the outside God coming to be inside. Now in verse four the emphasis shifts to that of permeating and saturating. It is something already present which is now moving into the whole being.

This is demonstrated in what is taking place in the lives of the disciples. There is only one explanation of the sudden ability to speak in languages they do not know. They have been invaded by the presence of another Being that is controlling and using them for the purposed plan of His design. Is this not a complete verification of our conclusion?

In his Gospel, Matthew records a discussion between

Jesus and His disciples. It is at the close of His Galilean ministry. A summary statement of Jesus' feeling about this ministry is given. He has seen the great multitudes *like sheep having no shepherd* (Matthew 9:36). He calls upon His disciples to pray for laborers for the harvest (Matthew 9:37-38). As they end their prayer, Jesus calls them as the answer to their prayer. He gives them power and they become apostles (Matthew 10:1-2). Before He releases them to minister, He gives them lengthy instructions. One part of that instruction is: *"But when they deliver you up, do not worry about how or what you should speak. For it will be given to you in that hour what you should speak; for it is not you who speak but the Spirit of your Father who speaks in you,"* (Matthew 10:19-20). If that was true in the early ministry of the apostles, how much more it is true now in the filling of the Holy Spirit! Can He become the source of my communication? Can he pervade my mind and spirit until nothing can be said with my tongue that will not be sourced by Him?

Luke continues in the verse by saying, *and began to speak* (Acts 2:4). The focus of the Greek word translated *speak* is not on the content of the speaking. It is the idea that the disciples uttered sounds which the hearers heard. This word is used in the sense of "to talk at random" contrasted with a speaking which involves the intellectual reason of man. Often this is used of children who talk and talk, but say nothing. Do you see this word strikes a blow at the foundation of the wisdom of man? My concern is not on the speaking, but on the content. What will I say? Will it make sense? Did I speak it correctly? How will it be received? This means I must be in control of what I am saying. I must figure it out and understand it thoroughly.

Something is happening to the tongues of the disciples which is completely beyond their reasoning and understanding. They are not in control of the content of their speaking. They are speaking in languages they do not know and therefore do not understand. A shift is being made in the lives of the disciples. The direction of the rudder determines their lives are changing sources. They will no longer be in control of their tongues, but the Spirit of Christ has invaded the deepest area of their lives. He will source even their speaking.

I want to be very plain about how strong I believe Luke is making this! Some one may say, "Well, my problem is I speak without thinking." Let me boldly say that this is not anyone's problem. That is not what is being advocated in this passage. Our speaking is not to be a product of our own thinking. There will be no difficulty in speaking if the Spirit of Christ pervades the depth of your mind and is in control of the rudder of your life. Listen closely again to the words of Jesus to His disciples. **"But when they deliver you up, do not worry about how or what you should speak. For it will be given to you in that hour what you should speak, for it is not you who speak but the Spirit of your Father who speaks in you,"** (Matthew 10:19-20).

Is it possible to be filled with the Spirit of Christ like this? Can I become so intimate with Him that my tongue is under His control? Is it possible for Him to pervade my mind and heart so even my tongue is sourced by Him? Is your Christianity "guarding, protecting, disciplining, and controlling," or is it, "relaxing, yielding, surrendering and dying? Is Christianity about doing it right and speaking correctly? Or is it about the filling of the Holy Spirit who becomes the controlling agent of my being? Does not this statement verify our conclusion? The Spirit of Jesus desires to permeate our faculties to produce through our tongue His message to our world. Will we let Him?

Let us return to our basic text. ***And they were all filled with the Holy Spirit and began to speak with other tongues...*** (Acts 2:4). The Greek word translated ***tongues*** is used at least fifty times in the New Testament. What is so interesting is the variety of usages it seems to have. It is used to refer to an organ of the body (Revelation 16:10). It is used in regard to taste (Luke 16:24). The tongue is often connected to the idea of speaking or the ability of speech (Mark 7:33-35). It is often personified (Romans 14:11; Philippians 2:11). It is used metaphorically to mean speech or language. This is the usage in our passage. This seems to be the area of controversy. It can refer to a particular language or dialect as spoken by a particular people (Acts 2:11; 1 Corinthians 13:1). But it can also refer to an "unknown" tongue (1 Corinthians 14:14).

It is clear from the study of the New Testament that there were two distinct uses of the word ***tongue*** in this regard. One was the promised gift of languages other than one's own native language. This was experienced by those who were filled with the Spirit of Pentecost. They affirm the Gospel among at least seventeen dialects on this great Day. However, this same word when used in the singular with a singular subject is translated "unknown tongue." It refers to the Corinthian practice of speaking in an unknown tongue not comprehended by anyone, and therefore, not an ordinary spoken language.

It is very clear which of these tongues is happening on the Day of Pentecost. The great crowds which heard the speaking *were all amazed and marveled, saying to one another, "Look, are not all these who speak Galileans? And how is it that we hear, each in our own language in which we were born?"* (Acts 2:7-8). The great concern of this Day of Pentecost was not in speaking in an unknown tongue, but in a known language.

Does this not verify our conclusion? The Spirit of Jesus desires to permeate our faculties in order to produce through our tongue His message to our world. Certainly this was accomplished in the first event of the filling of the Holy Spirit. Do we not see it continuing to be done throughout the book of Acts? Do we see it in our personal lives?

And they were all filled with the Holy Spirit and began to speak with other tongues, as the Spirit gave… (Acts 2:4). Luke is so concerned about the source of the speaking; he goes beyond the normal statement to emphasize the Holy Spirit who *gave.* The Greek word translated *gave* is used to speak of a person who does anything to or for another. It is one from whom anything is received, the source, author or cause. There is a definite emphasis on the "source." This word is often used in connection with God or of Christ as the author or source of what one has or receives. The Spirit of Christ furnished them with the content as well as with the language.

This Greek word is used four hundred and sixteen times in the New Testament. It is the ninth most frequently used verb. It is the most common expression for the procedure whereby a subject deliberately transfers something to someone or something so that it becomes available to the recipient. So you can see how strong Luke is in his emphasis of the Holy Spirit as the source! Luke gives no other explanation for what is taking place. There is not even a slight emphasis upon the disciples, but a total focus on the Spirit of Christ. Everything which is happening is a gift from Him.

We have already understood this concept from the example of Christ. The life Jesus lived was by God's gift. The Father gave Him His works (John 5:36). It was the Father who gave Him His disciples (John 6:37). Even His name was given by the Father (John 17:11). All things have been given into His hands (John 3:35). This strongly verifies our conclusion. The Spirit of Jesus desires to permeate our faculties in order to produce through our tongue His message to our world. There is no lack of resource or ability. There is no excuse! It is of Him and not of us.

We now come to the concluding part of our verse. ***And they were all filled with the Holy Spirit and began to speak with other tongues, as the Spirit gave them utterance*** (Acts 2:4). The Greek word which is translated ***utterance*** is in the infinitive mood. It is a verbal noun. In the English it is usually introduced with the word "to." It could be translated ***as the Spirit gave them*** "to utter." The purpose of this verbal noun is to fill out and give content to the main verb. Luke gives us a double emphasis to be sure we understand exactly what is happening. He tells us that ***the Spirit gave*** and ***the Spirit… uttered.*** Again he highlights the unity between the Spirit of Christ and the believer. The Spirit did not give to the believer and then the believer uttered. This would indicate division or separation between them. The Spirit acted through the believer.

This Greek word is two words put together. It is the

Greek word "apo" which is translated "from" and the Greek word meaning "to enunciate plainly or declare." This word is only used three times in the New Testament. All of these usages are in the Book of Acts. Luke uses this word to introduce Peter's sermon on the Day of Pentecost. ***But Peter, standing up with the eleven, raised his voice and said*** (uttered) ***to them,*** (Acts 2:14). Obviously Luke is using this word to indicate the clarity of Peter's message as he explains what is happening from the Book of Joel.

Luke uses this word in reference to the speaking of Paul. Festus was present when Paul defended himself before King Agrippa. Festus was so moved by Paul's defense that he cried out,

"Paul, you are beside yourself! Much learning is driving you mad!" But he (Paul) ***said, "I am not mad, most noble Festus, but speak*** (utter) ***the words of truth and reason,"*** (Acts 26:24-25).

On both of these occasions Luke specifically uses this word to emphasize clarity, and plainness of speaking. He stresses the issue of intelligible and meaningful words which we heard. This is also the meaning found in our verse (Acts 2:4). Our conclusion is verified once again. The Spirit of Jesus desires to permeate our faculties to produce through our tongue His message to our world. His message is plain and forceful. He will not leave our world in confusion. Will we become His mouth piece?

Is it possible to be so intimate with the Spirit of Jesus that even our tongue is under His control? He does not call us to speak in His behalf. He does not give us the message and we deliver it. This is not about obedience in that sense. He wants to unite with us in such a merging of beings that our tongue becomes His tongue. His mind becomes our mind. His will becomes our will. He is allowed to live His life through us. His life becomes our life. Oh, to be one with Him!

www.ingramcontent.com/pod-product-compliance
Lightning Source LLC
Chambersburg PA
CBHW071625040426
42452CB00009B/1486